Animals All Around

Do Frogs Have Fur?

A Book About Animal Coats and Coverings

by Michael Dahl

illustrated by Jeff Yesh

Special thanks to our advisers for their expertise:

Kathleen E. Hunt, Ph.D.
Research Scientist & Lecturer, Zoology Department
University of Washington, Seattle, Washington

Susan Kesselring, M.A., Literacy Educator
Rosemount-Apple Valley-Eagan (Minnesota) School District

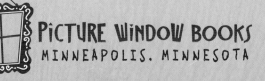
PICTURE WINDOW BOOKS
MINNEAPOLIS, MINNESOTA

Managing Editor: Bob Temple
Creative Director: Terri Foley
Editor: Peggy Henrikson
Editorial Adviser: Andrea Cascardi
Copy Editor: Laurie Kahn
Designer: Todd Ouren
Page production: BANTA Digital Group.
The illustrations in this book were rendered digitally.

Picture Window Books
5115 Excelsior Boulevard
Suite 232
Minneapolis, MN 55416
1-877-845-8392
www.picturewindowbooks.com

Printed in the United States of America.

Library of Congress Cataloging-in-Publication Data
Dahl, Michael.
Do frogs have fur? : a book about animal coats and coverings / by Michael Dahl ;
illustrated by Todd Ouren.
p. cm. — (Animals all around)
Includes bibliographical references and index.
ISBN 1-4048-0292-4 (lib. bdg.)
1. Body covering (Anatomy)—Juvenile literature. [1. Body covering (Anatomy) 2. Skin.]
I. Ouren, Todd, ill. II. Title.
QL942 .D24 2004
591.47'7—dc22
2003019151

Do frogs have fur?

No! Polar bears have fur.

A polar bear's fur keeps the bear toasty warm. The inner layer of fur is thick and woolly. The outer layer is made of hollow hairs. The bear's bright fur helps the animal blend in with the snow. Furry paws keep the polar bear from slipping on the ice.

Do frogs have feathers?

No! Cardinals have feathers.

A cardinal's coat has hundreds of feathers. Short, fluffy feathers next to its body keep the cardinal warm. Strong wing feathers help the cardinal fly. Stiff tail feathers help the bird steer as it flits and flies from tree to tree.

Do frogs have scales?

No! Fish have scales.

Slick, shiny scales lie flat along a fish's body. Some scales overlap like shingles on a roof. Some scales fit together like bricks in a wall. Water slides easily over the scales as the fish swims. Scales protect the fish's soft body when it bumps against rocks or bigger fish.

Do frogs have hair?

No! Horses have hair.

A horse is covered with a smooth coat of hair. The row of longer hair that grows along the top of a horse's head and neck is called a mane. A horse's tail sometimes has even longer hair. The horse can swish its tail and shake its mane to shoo away pesky flies.

Do frogs have fuzz?

No! Bumblebees have fuzz.

A fuzzy bumblebee lands on a flower. Powdery pollen inside the flower sticks to the bee's body. As the bee visits other flowers, some pollen falls off into the blossoms. The pollen helps make seeds for new flowers.

Do frogs have bristles?

13

No! Hedgehogs have bristles.

The back and sides of a hedgehog are covered in stiff, pointed bristles. This bristly coat keeps larger animals from eating the hedgehog. When it is frightened, the hedgehog rolls itself into a prickly ball.

Do frogs have outside skeletons?

No! Crayfish have outside skeletons.

A crayfish has a hard outer covering called an exoskeleton. As the crayfish grows, it gets too big for this shell. The animal then sheds its covering and eats it. The crayfish hides while it grows a bigger exoskeleton that will help protect it from enemies.

Do frogs have fleece?

No! Lambs have fleece.

Tight curls of fleece keep little lambs warm. When a lamb gets older, this soft, fluffy hair is cut off, and the lamb grows another coat. The fleece is called wool. It is spun into thread and yarn for making clothes and blankets to keep people warm.

Do frogs have shells?

No! Turtles have shells.

The painted turtle can pull its head and legs into its hard shell. The shell protects the turtle's soft body from the sharp beaks of hungry birds. The turtle can also hide inside its shell from enemies such as snakes and raccoons.

Do frogs have slimy skin?

Yes! Frogs have slimy skin.

A frog can soak up water and even breathe through its soft, thin skin. To breathe this way, the frog's skin must stay moist, even on land. A thin layer of slippery slime keeps the frog's skin from drying out when the frog leaves the water.

Animal Coats and Coverings

Some animals have soft coverings.

polar bears   fur

lambs   fleece

bumblebees   fuzz

Some animals have hard coverings.

hedgehogs   bristles

turtles   shells

crayfish   exoskeletons

Some animals have smooth coverings.

horses   hair

frogs   slimy skin

Some animals have coverings of many pieces.

cardinals   feathers

fish   scales

Glossary

bristle—a hard, thick, hair-like growth that is pointed and sharp

exoskeleton—a hard, bony covering on an animal

fleece—the coat of soft, fluffy hair covering a lamb or sheep

mane—the long hair that grows on the head and neck of some animals. Horses and lions have manes.

moist—a little bit wet

pollen—a powder made by flowers to help them create new seeds

scales—small pieces of tough skin that cover the bodies of some animals such as fish and snakes

wool—the soft, fluffy hair of a lamb or sheep. A coat of wool is called fleece.

Index

To Learn More

At the Library

Kee, Lisa Morris. *Whose Skin Is This? A Look at Animal Skin—Scaly, Furry, and Prickly.* Minneapolis: Picture Window Books, 2003.

Schwartz, David M. *Animal Feathers & Fur.* Milwaukee: Gareth Stevens Pub., 1999.

Schwartz, David M. *Animal Skin & Scales.* Milwaukee: Gareth Stevens Pub., 2000.

Zoehfeld, Kathleen Weidner. *What Lives in a Shell?* New York: HarperCollins Publishers, 1994.

On the Web

Fact Hound offers a safe, fun way to find Web sites related to this book. All of the sites on Fact Hound have been researched by our staff.
http://www.facthound.com

1. Visit the Fact Hound home page.
2. Enter a search word related to this book, or type in this special code: 1404802924.
3. Click on the FETCH IT button.

Your trusty Fact Hound will fetch the best sites for you!